ROMA

Author
Gerald R. Morgan

Translated by
Gareth Williams

Cardiff
University of Wales Press
1987

British Library Cataloguing in Publication Data

Morgan, Gerald, *1935-*
  Romans in Wales.
  1. Romans — Wales 2. Wales — Civilization
  I. Title II. Y Rhufeiniaid yng Nghymru.
  English
  936.2'904 DA715

  ISBN 0-7083-0960-7

ACKNOWLEDGEMENTS

The publishers would like to thank the following for
permission to reproduce photographs and for their
assistance.

Anne Mainman: frontispiece map, 17(G)

Roger Worsley: 2(B)

The Ermine Street Guard: 3(A), 18(H)

Glamorgan-Gwent Archaeological Trust: 4(C), 4(D),
  5(F), 6(G), 7(J), 9(P), 10(Q), 11(T), 23(A)

Aerofilms: 5(E), 14(C)

National Museum of Wales: 6(H), 7(K), 7(L), 8(M),
  8(N), 8(O), 10(R), 13(A) — the photograph, 14(B),
  16(E), 16(F)

The University of Newcastle-upon-Tyne: 10(S)

Nick Stuart: 13(A) — the sketch-plan

British Museum: 15(D)

University of Cambridge Press: 19(I)

D. Lyndon Howells: 20(J)

The Welsh Office: 23(B), 24(C)

CONTENTS

TIME-CHART OF MAIN EVENTS

55 BC	Julius Caesar's first expedition
54 BC	Julius Caesar's second expedition
AD 43	Roman conquest of Britain begins with the invasion of Aulus Plautius during the reign of the Emperor Claudius
AD 48	Attacks on Wales
AD 51	Caratacus taken prisoner
AD 60	Revolt led by Boudicca (Boadicea)
AD 74-78	Most of Wales conquered
AD 122	The Emperor Hadrian visits Britain
AD 230	The Saxons launch attacks on the east coast of Britain, followed later by attacks in the west from Ireland
AD 367	Attacks from the west, north and east. Roman Britain in decline
AD 407	The last Roman soldiers leave Britain
AD 410	The Emperor Honorius tells the inhabitants of Britain they must now fend for themselves

This book is based on an original Welsh title, *Y
Rhufeiniaid yng Nghymru.*

Printed in Wales by Graham Harcourt (Printers) Ltd.,
Swansea.

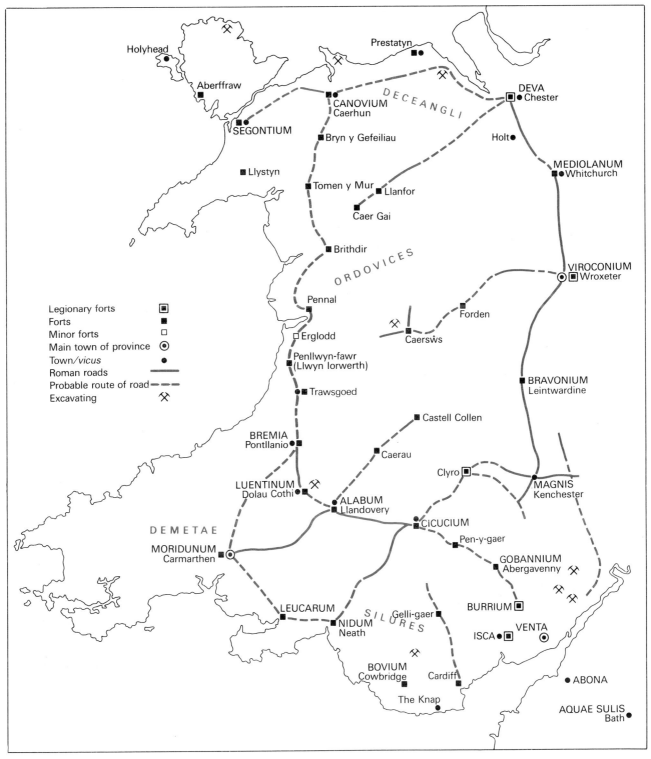

Holyhead

Aberffraw

Prestatyn

DECEANGLI

DEVA
Chester

CANOVIUM
Caerhun

SEGONTIUM

Bryn y Gefeiliau

Holt

MEDIOLANUM
Whitchurch

Llystyn

Tomen y Mur

Llanfor

Caer Gai

Brithdir

ORDOVICES

VIROCONIUM
Wroxeter

Pennal

Forden

Erglodd

Caersŵs

Penllwyn-fawr
(Llwyn Iorwerth)

BRAVONIUM
Leintwardine

Trawsgoed

Castell Collen

BREMIA
Pontllanio

Caerau

Clyro

LUENTINUM
Dolau Cothi

MAGNIS
Kenchester

ALABUM
Llandovery

CICUCIUM

DEMETAE

Pen-y-gaer

MORIDUNUM
Carmarthen

GOBANNIUM
Abergavenny

BURRIUM

LEUCARUM

SILURES

Gelli-gaer

NIDUM
Neath

ISCA

VENTA

BOVIUM
Cowbridge

Cardiff

ABONA

The Knap

AQUAE SULIS
Bath

Legionary forts
Forts
Minor forts
Main town of province
Town/vicus
Roman roads
Probable route of road
Excavating

Wales during the Roman period.

1

1. ROMAN REMAINS IN WALES

Most of you have probably seen books on the Romans. Some of them have been about Rome and the Roman World, others about the Romans in Britain. How do we find out about people who lived two thousand years ago?

Most of our information comes from the writings of the Romans themselves. For instance, we know that Julius Caesar came to Britain in 55 and 54 BC because he wrote an account of both expeditions. Similarly, we know the Romans began their conquest of Britain in AD 43 because a Greek named Dio Cassius described it, and it is the historian Tacitus we must thank for telling us about the revolt of Boudicca (Boadicea) in AD 60. Unfortunately, the Romans have little to say about Britain itself, so for further information we turn to the archaeologist.

The Romans tell us a great deal about their own daily life: their writings contain descriptions of their meals, their legal disputes, the kind of training they gave their soldiers and a host of other topics. But there is still more we would like to know about them and once again this is where the archaeologist can help.

THE ARCHAEOLOGIST AT WORK

An archaeologist is a man or woman who has been especially trained to unearth new information about the human past. Archaeology is such an enormous subject that no single person can hope to know everything, so archaeologists concentrate on becoming expert in a particular period. Some study Stone Age Man, or the Bronze or Iron Age, or the Greeks and the Romans; some will concentrate on the Egyptians, say, or the Middle Ages; others will specialize in what is known as industrial archaeology. They may be employed by government authorities, by museums or by universities, and they depend, too, on the help of people who are not professional archaeologists themselves but who have an interest in the subject and are only too willing to provide financial and practical assistance.

There are several aspects to the archaeologist's work. Though some will be fully occupied in digging and excavating, there is much more to it than that. Whatever is found has to be carefully examined, and the results are then published in a book or journal. Maps have to be drawn and photographs taken of the project. The objects found have to be scientifically analysed, arranged in order, and measures taken to ensure they will not deteriorate or crumble. Some archaeologists are interested in particular kinds of experiments, like building an Iron Age dwelling and living in it, or making pottery the way the Greeks did. There is a group of enthusiasts who are so fascinated by the Roman army that they have made armour and weapons for themselves and become quite expert on Roman military formation. They call themselves *The Ermine Street Guard*. **A**

We see them here in the armour of the period AD 50-100. The legionaries are ranked behind, while the three men in the foreground are: in the middle, the *centurio* (**centurion**), issuing orders; on the left, the *signifer* (standard-bearer), and on the right, the *cornicen* (horn-blower). Look how detailed their armour is.

GETTING STARTED

Since any likely remains are buried under layer upon layer of earth, how does the archaeologist know where to start digging? Occasionally, of course, the remains are plainly visible, like the Roman walls at Caerleon and Caer-went which still stand, proud and dignified, for all to see. But there are occasions, too, when 'obvious' remains can deceive. One archaeologist has described excavating a mound that looked like an ancient burial — but it turned out to be no more than a refuge made by a farmer for his cows when the nearby river flooded its banks! Some things can also give the impression of being Roman when they are not. For instance, the little bridge between Swansea and Oystermouth, or the 'Roman steps' near Harlech **B** are not at all of Roman construction in reality.

B

A

An archaeological site can be discovered in various ways, and the first we will mention is — finding one accidentally! Workmen may be digging a trench and quite by chance come across bones, or a dish, or fragments of a **mosaic**. When this happens, it is essential that the authorities are informed and digging is suspended until archaeologists can be called in to inspect the site and excavate it further if necessary. Many an important discovery has been made like this: by the workmen who came across some Roman remains on a building site in Llandough, for example. What do you think is about to happen in C?

C

Archaeologists have to be prepared to do a fair amount of leg-work, and as they have been trained to detect indications and traces of past life both on the flat and on high ground, they often see things that most of us would fail to notice. A man called Ivan Margary was extremely good at this: for many years he followed the track of Britain's Roman roads and uncovered many that were previously unknown. A good deal of this kind of work still needs to be done in Wales, as it is certain that there are more Roman roads to be discovered here. You can see two roads in the photo of Cowbridge. D What is the main difference between the Roman road and the modern dual carriageway?

The third principal method of discovering new archaeological sites is by studying aerial photographs. E This can be very rewarding since all kinds of features are visible from the air that may not be apparent at ground level. Sometimes these can only be made out in the snow, or during a prolonged dry spell: in the hot summer of 1976 two new Roman

forts were found in north Ceredigion at Llwyn Iorwerth and Erglodd. A newly-developed technique of taking photographs from the air is to use a special type of film that receives infra-red rays and can as a result reveal features that are invisible to the naked eye and that do not show up on an ordinary film.

The archaeologist will do field-work, or fly over a certain area with his camera at the ready, because he already suspects the existence of some kind of site in that locality. This is precisely how the sites at Erglodd, Llwyn Iorwerth and Trawsgoed were discovered, between the already-known forts at Pontllanio and Pennal. Historians had long been puzzled by a gap in their maps where they thought some evidence *should* exist. Intensive and patient field-work eventually uncovered what they were looking for, the missing link in the chain. Clearly, map-making and field-work are vitally important aspects of archaeology.

The most recently-developed technique of searching for archaeological sites is by the use of special instruments. A site will occasionally be discovered as the result of the sound emitted by a metal-detector when it finds a piece of metal in the ground. Archaeologists do not recommend the use of these particular devices because people cannot resist digging out the object detected, often with disregard for anything else. That is why metal-detectors are banned from sites already known to the authorities. But trained archaeologists themselves do employ electrical instruments to help locate walls and ditches.

D

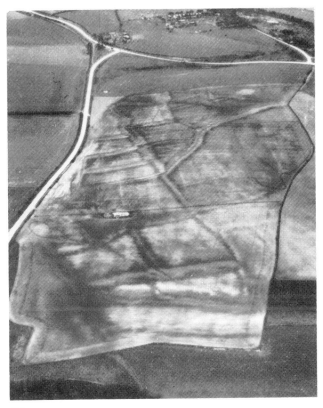

The outline of Celtic fields can be seen in this view of Chilcomb Down.

EXCAVATING

People have excavated ancient sites for centuries, mainly in the hope of discovering hidden treasure, but in their search for gold and silver they have often destroyed a great deal of historical evidence. During this century archaeologists have sought not treasure-trove, but information. Yet even they can make mistakes, and it is always in the back of their minds that they could be ruining a site in the very process of excavating it. So extreme caution is called for.

The basis of scientific excavation is stratigraphy, the study of strata. The earth beneath our feet generally lies in layers, as you can see in any vegetable garden. On the surface the soil is light and fertile, but underneath is a layer of heavier, less fertile soil and beneath that again, rock or clay. The deeper we dig, the further back in time we are likely to be going.

We say 'likely to be' because there are many exceptions to the rule: it does not always follow that the lower layer is older than the one above it. Consider, for instance, a site where people of the Neolithic period built a fort. They live there for some length of time then they move away, leaving it empty. Hundreds of years later the Romans arrive there and dig a ditch or sink a deep well. The bottom of the well will be lower than the fort, but not as old.

So as he excavates, the archaeologist has to record the layers, or strata, very carefully, and note every detail. By working in this way, he hopes to be able to arrange his evidence in **chronological order**.

THE EVIDENCE

What kind of things does the archaeologist of a Roman site in Wales hope to discover? The question is a simple one, but the answer is complex.

First of all he or she will hope, by excavating, to find the layer of soil dating from the Roman period. If, for example, he has penetrated a Roman earthwork he may find the original layer beneath the material used to build it.

With luck he may then be able to take samples of the soil and send them for a laboratory test. There, analysts will separate what seeds they find in the soil, as well as pollen and other traces of other plant life of that area as it was in the Roman period. They will then have an idea of how the landscape looked and will be able to suggest what trees were common or rare in the region, and what sort of corn was grown. They will also discover traces of insects and other small creatures, thus enabling us to understand more of the environment in former times.

Naturally the archaeologist digs in the hope that he will encounter the remains of some kind of building. He may be searching for the outline of a military fort, or for particular buildings within it. At the present time archaeologists are excavating the enormous bath-house built for the Roman legionaries at Caerleon. On Holyhead Mountain on Anglesey, they recently found the remains of a Roman tower that was possibly a watch-tower to look out for pirates. One of the most exciting discoveries of recent times is the large 22-room building that has come to light at The Knap, Barry, F and G. No one is quite sure what its purpose was. Do you have any suggestions?

5

fragments of pottery, coins, human and animal bones, glass, items made out of iron (like nails and carpenter's materials), bronze (jewellery, pins) and such like.

If the archaeologist is very fortunate, his finds will include an inscription, that is, a fragment of stone or hard clay with words and letters on it. The most interesting, but the rarest, are those from public buildings. One of these was found in Caerleon in marble, and is one of the finest of its kind in Britain. Unfortunately, although we know this inscription dates from the year AD 100, we do not know on what building it was put up. The stone had later been used as a slab in the pavement of a storeroom! Here is a picture of it: H

H

G

We tend to think of Roman buildings as being made of stone, but many were of timber construction like the Roman quay discovered near Caerleon on the River Usk. Timber fragments were also found in the small fort at Brithdir near Dolgellau, the remains of some fairly small building like a tanning-pit perhaps. The most that the archaeologist will often come across are the sockets for what must have been wooden posts, or small trenches that provided the foundations for stone walls — except that each and every stone has been removed over the centuries to make a well or some other construction.

Once the archaeologist has begun to expose an actual building he must be extremely careful. He may now discover that the Romans had altered it by building new walls or doors in some places or by dismantling parts of it in others. The experienced archaeologist can detect structural alterations of this kind. Sometimes he will need to pull down part of, or even an entire, wall in order to get at a still older section.

There is no telling what kind of remains the archaeologist may actually find in the course of digging but, depending to some extent on the location, he or she would hope to come across

Some of the words have been abbreviated. The inscription in full reads: I

I

IMPERATORI CESARI DIVI NERVAE
FILIO NERVAE TRAIANO AUGUSTO
GERMANICO PONITIFICI MAXIMO
TRIBUNICA POTESTATE PATRI PATRIAE
CONSULI III
LEGIO II AUGUSTA

Its translation is: (Erected for) The Emperor Caesar Nerva Traianus, son of Nerva the Divine, Augustus, Conqueror of Germany, Chief Priest, Tribunician, Father of his Country, Consul for the third time. The Second Augstan Legion.

Inscriptions can vary. Some (like that of Julius Valens on p.22) are gravestones. The name of a military unit on a stone or tile indicates that the unit had been building there. Other inscriptions may be shrines to the gods. Equally interesting from the archaeologist's point of view are pieces of crockery with words on them, and curse-tablets (lead coins with curses inscribed on them) are fascinating too. Why do you think they were thrown into a well?

As you might expect, Roman coinage is a vast subject. A coin's value to the archaeologist is that it helps him in the work of dating, for unless the coin is in poor condition it is possible to put an actual date on it, providing great care is taken. The fact that a coin is found lying in a certain layer of earth does not necessarily mean that the earth at that point is of the same age as the coin, which might have fallen into a mousehole! But if the coin is found in a vessel or under a stone, it is quite possible that it can then assist the archaeologist in the work of dating. Again, caution is called for — it needs careful examination to see whether it is worn or in mint condition. J

Fragments of pottery are found on most Roman sites, and they too can be of great assistance to the archaeologist. Just as fashions change in the world of pottery today, so too did they in Roman times. A particularly popular kind during the first two centuries AD was a hard, red, glossy type made in Gaul and known as Samian pottery. K

K

It is possible to date this kind of pottery fairly accurately, which helps the archaeologist a great deal. The stamp of its manufacturers Severus and Pudens was found on a piece of pottery discovered near Carmarthen castle, and we know that they were in business between AD 65 and 85. Of course, it is possible that somebody had preserved this vessel for many years, but the likelihood in this instance is that it reached Carmarthen fairly early on.

This is far from being the only piece of Roman pottery in Britain that we know of, though. There were important pottery-works in and around the New Forest, in Oxford and in the Nene Valley, while in photo L we see a lamp made in the kilns of the Twentieth Augustan Legion at Holt on the River Dee. What is particularly interesting is that the manufacturer has falsely stamped it with the name Fortis, a firm in northern Italy!

L

As we can see from photo M the Romans were fine glass-makers too. This is a glass vessel of the first century AD from Caerleon, later used to keep the ashes of a cremated body. The archaeologist always feels a certain excitement when he finds a burial site, especially if a body has been interred there. Cremation graves are less interesting as it is then impossible to tell the age or sex of the dead person, or the cause of death. But when a mass burial-ground containing hundreds of skeletons is found, scientists can learn a great deal about life and death in the Roman era.

Animal bones also aid the archaeologist, since they give him an idea as to which farm animals were common, what pets people kept, and what they were fed on. All kinds of animal bones may turn up, that had once been cows, sheep, deer, goats, horses, cats and dogs. In Roman times animal bones served a number of useful purposes and archaeologists have come across all kinds of objects made out of bone, including knife-handles, combs, hairpins, needles, and dice. Animal hides were also used to make leather goods like shoes, bracelets, bags, hats, harnesses and tents, for however wet the surroundings, leather is very durable and does not rot.

M

O

Bronze and iron are the metals most commonly found on Roman sites in Wales, or anywhere else. Silver and gold are extremely rare, which is why Caerleon's greatest treasure is the silver decoration found in 1928 that was once part of a military standard N. An equally priceless object found at

Segontium near Caernarfon is a gold armlet with Greek lettering on it which was meant to protect the wearer from misfortune and evil spells. Photograph O shows a bronze jug found in Welshpool. Notice its handle, which is in the form of the legendary hero Hercules as a boy.

N This piece of solid silver was probably the pointed tip of a *signum*, the legionary standard.

Many of the bronze objects found on Roman sites are simple pieces of jewellery, while those made of iron tend to be everyday items like nails, tools for carpentry, farming and gardening, items of armour and various weapons. On the site of a fort at Inchtuthil in Scotland archaeologists found a thousand nails buried in the ground. Can you think why they may have been left in this way?

P Llandough *villa*.

Two items commonly found on site are plasterwork and pieces of mosaic, which are indications that there had once been houses standing there. Not everybody could afford mosaic floors which were rarely to be found outside the town houses and country *villae* of the wealthy. There are only four *villae* known in Wales: in Llanfrynach in Powys, in Ely and in Llandough, near Cardiff, and near Llantwit Major in the Vale of Glamorgan, P and Q. The site near Llantwit is really interesting: little excavating has been done there as yet and archaeologists are quite content to leave it as it is. Since the site is in no danger, they hope that further developments in excavation methods will enable them to unearth more information in the future. We still would like to know more about *villae*, such as how much land was attached to them, and what sort of people their owners were.

R

Not much in the way of mosaic work has come to light in Wales, unfortunately. It was a form of decoration that the Romans adopted from the Greeks, who had themselves learnt it from the East. It was obtained by craftsmen using local stone to form the various colours found in the designs and patterns. In southern England they used chalk and limestone for white, marble for blue and grey, sandstone for yellow and brown, and *terracotta* (fire-hardened clay) for red. The mosaic in R comes from the military headquarters at Caerleon.

So far we have been talking about the discoveries an archaeologist would expect to make. There are times, however, when more unexpected and diverse items are unearthed. The bottom of a well at Segontium, for instance, was found to contain pieces of timber that had once formed barrel staves: surprisingly, they had not rotted away over the centuries. In fact, where the earth is wet the archaeologist can often hope to find something unexpected beneath.

Just such a location in Britain is Vindolanda on Hadrian's Wall where, in March 1973, a startling discovery was made. An archaeologist named Robin Birley was clearing away the mud from the bottom of a cold, wet ditch and found underneath a lot of straw, bracken and scraps of wood. Among these he found some small narrow wooden slivers with ink markings on them. They proved to be writing tablets, and further digging soon unearthed 202 such pieces, with markings on most of them. You can see one in photo S.

S

These fragile little tablets were taken to a laboratory to be preserved, though only after ensuring that the ink would not fade when exposed to the open air and that the wood would not dry up and shrivel. The next step was to find experts who could decipher the markings on them. It turned out that some of these tablets were private letters, and the rest were official documents like lists of payment for food. From these lists we can learn what the Romans ate when they were in Britain. They mention barley, fish sauce, pork fat, vegetables, salt, vintage and sour wines, beer, goat meat, young pig, ham and venison. One of Britain's governors is mentioned in one letter, and there are references to everyday things like warm underwear. Before finding these tablets, we never knew Roman soldiers wore such things! In addition, scholars have been able to learn a great deal about the language and writing methods used by people of that time. Many more such tablets are likely to come to light in the future, but it is a fair bet that archaeologists fifty years ago would not have spotted those little wooden slivers, nor recognised their significance.

T

As we said earlier, digging and excavating is only part of the archaeologist's work. Once a site is discovered, his or her work is really endless. Each bears a heavy responsibility because very delicate items are now in their trust, and they have to ensure they are properly preserved. In T, a stone-mason is helping archaeologists at The Knap, Barry, by strengthening the walls. Because it is very costly to open a site to the public, there are times when the archaeologist has to decide whether to re-bury it. On the other hand, once the decision has been made to open a site up, the archaeologist has to consider the members of the public who will be likely to visit it. Should some of the site be restored so that sight-seers will be better able to appreciate what they are looking at?

Everything that is discovered on the site is stored in orderly fashion and sometimes displayed in a museum or an exhibition open to all. Detailed information relating to the site is then published in a book or learned journal, or even in a handy brochure.

Our ideas and knowledge about the Romans are constantly changing and improving. It is less than twenty years ago, for instance, that archaeologists decided that Moridunum was not a Roman fort after all, but a town, one that was probably the capital of the Demetae, a native tribe of Dyfed.

It is highly likely that in years to come archaeology will shed still more light on Roman activities in Wales. Further military forts may be discovered, another town and — who knows — perhaps a couple of new *villae*. We may even find an inscription bearing the Roman name for Cardiff! But in the long run such major discoveries are less important than the painstaking field-work and careful digging that goes on every year and which adds to our knowledge slowly and surely.

WHAT CAN YOU DO?

Where can you find out more about archaeology? First of all you can read further on the topic — there have been many books written about the Romans, and about the Romans in Britain. It is more difficult to obtain information about their activities in Wales, but the publications that can be bought at the museums in Caerleon, Segontium and elsewhere provide an excellent introduction.

Secondly, you can join 'The Young Archaeologists' Club' which publishes a quarterly magazine called *Young Archaeology*, obtainable from Dr Kate Pretty, New Hall, Cambridge, CB3 0DF. Perhaps you can also persuade your school to subscribe to the University of Sheffield project, *Archaeology in Education* by writing to the Department of Prehistory and Archaeology at the University of Sheffield. In Wales the Glamorgan-Gwent Archaeological Trust welcomes groups of young enthusiasts to their centre at 6 Prospect Place, South Dock, Swansea. Why not pay a visit?

There are hundreds of archaeological journals, but most of them are written by and for specialists. The one likely to be of most interest to the general reader is *Popular Archaeology* — inquire at your newsagent or write directly to 24 Barton Street, Bath. It is sometimes possible for young people to help at a 'dig' but you need to bear a few things well in mind before doing so. In the first place the work can be cold, wet, tiring and tedious for lengthy periods! Secondly, if you make a promise to help, keep to it. Thirdly, do not expect to get paid. And finally, the opportunity you may be given could be on a site dating from an altogether different period, even though your own interest is in the Romans. But it is still a good idea to do it because you will learn a great deal about archaeological techniques that will stand you in good stead later.

We can conclude this section by insisting on two things quite firmly: one, never try digging by yourself; and two, never use a metal-detector on any site of historical interest.

And a final word. If you are thinking of becoming a professional archaeologist, you will need to go to university and study Archaeology either as a single subject or in combination with others. It is also a good idea to do French, German and Latin to fifth form examination level at least, and some Chemistry too. There are more than 1,200 professional archaeologists in Britain today — but we could do with even more!

2. MILITARY LIFE AT CAERLEON

EARLY MORNING

It is a little before dawn, on the fourteenth day before the April Kalends, in the year 883 since the founding of Rome, the thirteenth year of the reign of the Emperor Hadrian Ⓐ — or according to our calendar, 19 March in the year of Our Lord (AD) 130. But, naturally enough, Gaius Julius Valens knows nothing of our calendar. As a soldier serving in the **province** of Britannia (Britain), far from Rome, he is unlikely to have heard of Our Lord Jesus Christ at all.

It is getting lighter in the east, but Valens and seven other soldiers are still sleeping soundly on their straw pallets, each wrapped in his woollen cloak. The room is small and stuffy. As dawn breaks, the green glass in the window allows in just sufficient light for us to make out the men more clearly.

The room is one of a row in the same barracks in the corner of the military fort of Isca (Caerleon, today) which is situated near the river Isca (Usk, today). In the room there are soldiers sleeping. There is a door opposite the window in each room, and beyond the door another small room where various pieces of equipment are carefully laid out. A leather tent occupies one corner, and there are also soldiers' armour and weapons as well as things like a saw, an axe, a sickle, a hammer, a length of rope, a spade and a basket. There are also two large, flat stones lying one on top of another: these are the millstones which grind the grain into flour.

At the far end of the long, narrow building are a number of rooms separate from the others. In one of these sleeps the centurion Quintus Valerius Felix, to give him his full name. 'Felix' means 'happy' or 'fortunate', but behind his back the soldiers have other names for him they think suit him better! Felix is an officer, a centurion responsible for eighty men. Physically tough, he has a voice like a rasp and a temper like fury. The soldiers fear him — if they displease him he may beat them with his **vine-staff** — but they envy him too, for he earns five thousand *denarii* a year, at least five times their own pay. Furthermore, any soldier hoping for some kind of favour from Felix will have to pay him for it.

The fort and barracks in Isca are similar to any others the length and breadth of the Roman Empire. Soldiers like Valens and centurions like Felix carry similar weapons, are paid in the same kind of money, receive the same military training and speak the same language, whether they are serving in Britain, Spain, Gaul, Africa, Asia Minor, Greece, Syria or Palestine. There are hundreds of forts throughout the Roman world, but fewer than fifty are as big as Isca, because it is the base-camp of the Second Augustan Legion.

The fort is there to ensure peace and enforce order in this region of the province of Britain. The country is not yet called 'Wales' nor do the inhabitants call themselves 'Welsh'. The name given by the Romans to the district around Isca is **Civitas** Silurum. The *Silures* are the local Celtic inhabitants. They were fierce opponents of the Romans and fought to resist every attempt to take possession of their lands west of the river Sabrina (the Severn). But when, fifty years ago, the Roman army reached the banks of the Isca and began the construction of their massive fort, the Silures gave up their struggle. They had lost their best men and their leaders had fled or been killed.

Although Valens, Felix and the rest of the **century** are still asleep, some of the soldiers in the fort are awake. They have been on night sentry duty, on the look-out for attack — though it is fifty years or more since the Silures last launched an attack on the Romans. They have to watch out for thieves too. We can see a sentry parading the wall alongside Felix's barracks, approaching the near gate where the centurion of the night-watch awaits him. The sentry's name is Longinus, and he stops every so often to peer out through the morning mist towards the west, and listens. It is vital he stays awake, for if the centurion caught him nodding he would beat him about the back and the arms with his vine-staff, and maybe take him to face an officer. This might result in Longinus being forced to live on water and barley alone for a period of time. And if it were also discovered, after he had been caught, that there *were* enemies in the vicinity, the other soldiers might beat him to death.

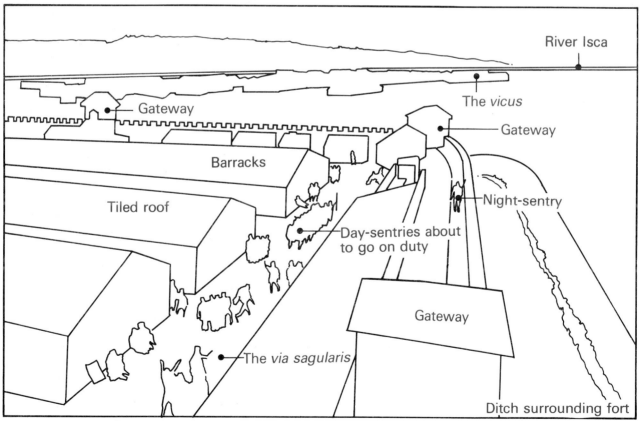

Gateway

The *vicus*

River Isca

Gateway

Barracks

Night-sentry

Tiled roof

Day-sentries about
to go on duty

Gateway

The *via sagularis*

Ditch surrounding fort

A

[B] The *basilica* and *forum* at Caer-went. The *basilica* (the building with the twin doors) was the town hall and the *forum* (which fills the other three sides) was the market place. This is where the people are heading.

Let us join Longinus on the wall and watch the fort come to life. The sky is reddening in the east and light creeps over fields that in the summer will grow corn for the soldiers. Ten miles to the east lies the town of Venta, the only town in the region where Silures who have become Romanized live. [B] To the south Longinus can see the dark shadow of the Isca river and the quay where the ships are moored.

Between the fort and the river Longinus can make out the dark outline of the **amphitheatre** [C] and, nearer, the parade-ground where the soldiers drill and do their military exercises. At the far end of the parade-ground he can see the roofs of cottages, craftsmen's workshops, and the shops and taverns that make up the *vicus*. This is the civilian settlement, where the soldiers go to relax and where their wives and families live. If the soldier is not on night duty, he can of an evening or a day off leave the fort for the *vicus* to drink, play dice and enjoy better food than the usual military rations. In law the soldier does not have the right to marry, but if he takes a fancy to one of the local girls he can set up home for his unofficial family in a cottage in the *vicus*. He is not allowed formally to marry until he has completed his 25-year service, and if he is transferred to another fort he is expected to leave his family behind. They may follow him if they wish, but they will not receive any official assistance to help them do so.

[C] Some idea of the size of the amphitheatre may be gained from this picture of its remains today.

14

Longinus has a wife and children living in the *vicus* and he will head there rather than go back to barracks to sleep once his watch is over. He turns his gaze now from the *vicus* and looks back towards the east, across the fort itself. It is huge — 40 acres of land enclosed by rectangular walls. By now some sections of these have been entirely rebuilt of stone, while others are still made of the original turf and timber construction. In each wall there is a massive gateway.

Felix and his men's barracks are very near to us, and we can see twenty-five similar buildings, extending in pairs for a quarter of a mile across the fort. Over there we can see some of the important buildings that occupy the centre of the fort — the drill-hall, the house of the **legatus** and the headquarters. We cannot see the granaries, the workshops, the hospital or the bath-house, but they are there all the same, and beyond them another twenty-six barracks.

We can see that the lower sections of Felix's barracks are made of stone, and the upper parts of timber and plaster, which in turn support reddish tiles. Between the ramparts and the barracks is a roadway which runs all around the fort just inside the walls; this is known as the **via sagularis**, the 'cloak street'. And we can see up against the defensive wall itself the kitchen huts and the latrines.

A bugle sounds from somewhere in the centre of the fort and others respond from the four main gates. Longinus, his shift over, hurries to the nearest gateway and with the other tired night-sentries forms up in the street under the watchful eye of the centurion. Opposite, the day-sentries are about to take over as the new centurion salutes the night-duty officer. Then the soldiers are dismissed. Some disperse to their barracks, others leave the fort in the direction of the *vicus*. Longinus is among them, and Regina will be glad to see him.

Back in Felix's barracks, however, all is noise and commotion. The fiery centurion is on his feet, barking at everyone to get up. Valens makes haste to fold his nightgown and the straw pallet he has been sleeping on, dons his simple tunic and hurries out to the latrines. These consist of a row of unpartitioned seats cut out of a long bench, beneath which running water carries the waste to an underground pipe that empties into the river half a mile away. The soldiers sit and talk there for a while, maybe sharing the odd joke, before going back out into the fresh air.

Out in the street, Felix's soldiers form up in groups of eight. After roll-call, Felix issues his instructions. Some of the men are told they are on duty in the barracks with the job of cleaning and sweeping out the soldiers' rooms, including Felix's own quarters. He will expect to find clean water in his cooking pot, charcoal ready for his heater, and his armour and weapons gleaming.

Others are detailed to bring water, get a fire going under the kitchen oven, collect the day's rations, and grind the corn with the quern, or hand-mill. Still others will have to sweep the outside of the barracks — the floor, the road and the latrines. The remainder of the soldiers report to the headquarters to receive their orders from the officer of the day. You will have noticed that the soldiers do not have breakfast — that is the Roman custom.

THE MORNING'S WORK

You may be rather surprised that the soldiers are not getting ready to fight a battle somewhere — after all, isn't that what soldiers are for? Maybe, but there are few wars being fought at the present time and Britain is relatively peaceful. So while the troops are not allowed to neglect their drill, their time is fully taken up by day-to-day activities, and while Valens and seven others report to headquarters for the day-officer's instructions, the rest buzz around like bees as they go about their various morning tasks. The fort is far from crowded, for all that: many of the five thousand or more soldiers that are in the legion are elsewhere. Hundreds are in the north of the province helping to construct the remarkable coast-to-coast wall that Hadrian has ordered built. D. The Emperor came to Britain eight years ago when Valens was a trainee soldier, and the excitement and expectation that ran through the camp as they prepared for the imperial visit to Isca remains vivid in his memory to this day.

D The Emperor Hadrian.

15

E

F

For that matter, Valens will always remember the year he spent working on that same wall, supervising the slaves who were digging the enormous foundation-trench and breaking the stones in the quarries. The weather was so bitter he wore thick socks and warm underclothes the whole time he was up there, and was certainly glad to get back to Isca.

As well as those soldiers working on the northern wall, there are others elsewhere, improving the roads in the west, repairing bridges and helping to build the smaller forts of Burrium, Cicucium, Nidum and Leucarum. You may be surprised at all the construction work that soldiers are expected to do, but two points are worth bearing in mind.

One is that every large army has to build roads, bridges and do all kinds of technical work, just as the Royal Engineers do in the British Army today. The second point to make is that there were two kinds of soldier in the Roman army — the **legionary** E and the **auxiliary** F.

A legionary like Valens is a Roman citizen, and receives training not only in warfare but in construction and maintenance work as well. The auxiliary is not a Roman citizen, and skilled work is not expected of him as it is of the legionary. We might add that an auxiliary receives much less when he has completed his military service: he is rewarded with Roman citizenship, while the legionary is given land to farm. The auxiliaries, too, are front-line troops who bear the brunt of battle, while the legionaries hold back to intervene if things get desperate.

By now Valens and his companions have lined up in front of the *Principia* (headquarters), which will be a massive building when it is finally completed. Three sides of the enclosed central courtyard are occupied by rooms and **armouries**, while at the far end is a long hall with a raised platform from which the commanding officer addresses his troops. Behind the hall are the offices where the administrative work of the fort is carried out. All the various papers and documents relating to every single soldier are filed here — his pay and terms of service, the details of every building project currently in progress throughout the legionary district, a record of all the provisions kept in stock. The papers are in the care of clerks who also deal with all the official correspondence that is delivered by road-messengers throughout the whole length and breadth of the Empire.

In a central position among these offices is a chamber where the legion's most valued possessions are held — the Eagles. These are the legionary standards that are kept at the shrine of the god Augustus and taken out once a year on the legion's anniversary — 23 September by our calendar — when all the soldiers form up on the parade ground, looking spick and span.

Valens knows these buildings very well; after all, he helped build the offices and the hall even if the work remains unfinished. Today, however, the day-officer (a young man from Rome, of a wealthy family and oozing self-confidence) gives him orders to work in the hospital, G. This comes as something of a surprise to Valens, since there has not been any fighting recently and more than half the building is closed.

Still, the hospital is a fine new one as he well knows, having worked here, too, two years ago. In the middle of it is an attractive herb-garden where there are all kinds of plants used for medicinal purposes — wormwood, milfoil, St John's wort, burdock and such like. Few are in flower at the moment as this is still only March.

By the time Valens reaches the hospital there is a queue of soldiers outside seeking treatment for various minor ailments. One or two have dental trouble, some have had accidents while building, others feel feverish. Still others want their eyes treated for a painful redness that afflicts them known as 'pink-eye', a common ailment in the winter and spring months especially. Neither Valens nor the best qualified doctors in Rome know what causes it, though today specialists attribute it to diet deficiency, notably in vitamins.

Valens' task is not to look after the sick but to assist the head doctor, a Greek by the name of Andronicos. He has orderlies to provide him with medical assistance, but Valens has to supervise the native servants who clean the rooms and take important messages. Andronicos is already at work in his room, treating patients. Valens pauses a minute to admire his skill in extracting a tooth from the first soldier in the queue. One of the orderlies is helping to hold the man down: there is only wine to ease the pain and the tough Roman writhes in agony as the doctor goes to work on him with his pliers.

G

The sick-rooms occupy three sides of the building that encloses the herb-garden, with a corridor dividing them into outer and inner wards. There are two cubicles for each military unit, but since many of the troops are serving some distance away, part of the hospital is empty. Two youths from the *vicus* are waiting for Valens. Their task is to sweep, wash and clean out the corridor, and Andronicos will be looking in to inspect their work by midday — he is a stickler for keeping his hospital clean and tidy.

Valens likes the hospital — it is quiet and always smells fresh. Fortunately for him he has never seen it in wartime, when it is overflowing with bloodied and badly injured soldiers swearing, roaring and groaning in agony as the doctors amputate a leg here, an arm there. Today, though, Valens has an opportunity to chat with his friend Aurelius.

Aurelius is suffering from acute rheumatic pains and fears that his military career may be over. A soldier is of little value to his country if he is a virtual cripple for most of the winter and unable to walk without crutches. But Andronicos is doing his best to cure it, keeping him in hospital and arranging for him to attend the bath-house next door every day.

Today Aurelius is really excited. He is determined to get permission to leave Isca for a while in order to go for treatment in the hot baths at Aquae Sulis. He is quite prepared to spend all his savings and he has booked a place on a boat that will take him from the river Isca across the Sabrina to the Abona (Avon). Fortunately, Aquae Sulis is not far from the sea. Andronicos has promised to write a letter on his behalf to one of the doctors at the temple of the goddess Minerva.

Valens recognizes one or two of the other soldiers in the hospital. If they have a temperature or are feverish, there is a good chance Andronicos will be able to cure them with herbal remedies and by insisting they eat the right food. But he cannot perform any real surgery because there is nothing like anaesthetic in existence. So some internal disorder such as dysentery can be fatal.

By midday Valens has satisfied himself that the corridor and the cubicles are clean, has delivered an important message and is now free to return to barracks. As he crosses the *via praetoria*, the main street, he has to wait for a yoke of draught-oxen pulling carts to pass. One is loaded with new tiles from the large pottery-works some distance away, another with stones, and the third with grain.

MILITARY TRAINING

After a light meal of porridge washed down with the local brew (the new wine is not yet ready to drink), Valens reports to Felix to receive his instructions for the afternoon — if there are any, for he is secretly hoping it will be free. To his disappointment, he and nine others have to accompany the centurion to the parade-ground where some young soldiers are to be given military exercises; and Felix always expects his men to work hard. H

H The centurion Felix issues instructions to his men.

On the parade-ground, a centurion hands over responsibility for the eighty trainees he is drilling to Felix. They are between 16 and 20 years old, strapping specimens of young manhood from Spain and Gaul. Felix begins by marching them up and down from one end of the parade-ground to the other to see how well they understand commands in Latin and whether they can march and wheel in step.

Then they all move down to one end of the parade-ground where there is a row of stout, wooden posts. It is Valens' job to supervise four young soldiers who are taking it in turns to engage the post in 'combat'. Each one carries a heavy shield and wooden sword, and he has to imagine the post is an opponent to be dealt blows around the head and legs while protecting his own body at the same time. If the trainee seems merely to be swiping ineffectively

at the dummy, he earns a sharp reprimand from Valens for failing to inflict crippling and, ideally, fatal injuries.

He will get another tongue-lashing from him if he uses his shield incorrectly. The shield is meant not only to protect the body but to drive one's opponent back as well. After the four have each engaged in further weapon practice on the wooden dummy, they divide into pairs and fight one another with wooden swords until they are soon bathed in perspiration and covered in bruises. Then Felix calls them together and splits them up into two opposing groups, a small group of 'Roman' soldiers and a larger one of 'barbarians' who use staves rather than swords. The air is filled with shouts and exclamations as Valens and the other instructors urge them on to greater efforts.

Ⅱ Laying a Roman road, closely supervised by a centurion.

Valens well remembers his own period of training — months of drill and exercises, cross-country marching with loads of stones, not to build walls but to build up bodies! A legionary may still be required to undertake such tasks, but whereas a young soldier is nervous and unsure of himself early on, he will learn from experience that they are not so impossible after all, even on a day's march of 25 miles.

Before long the young trainees would be heading through the mountains to Cicucium, sleeping in tents and learning how to build a temporary fort by day. They will have to mark out the perimeter, dig a ditch and pile up the earth into a rampart, make a fence from stakes and brushwood, put up their leather tents and fetch water, with the centurion driving them remorselessly all the while. They will sleep like logs and be up again in no time, to fold their tents, pull up the fence and keep moving for another day.

A craft took longer to learn than military skills. Soldiers spent months in the workshops and quarries working with wood, stone and metal. They learned how to build a bridge from timber, first on dry land, then across a stream, and finally across a river. In the

process they might fall in, which is why being able to swim had been one of the first things they were made to learn in their first few months in the army.

Next came road-building 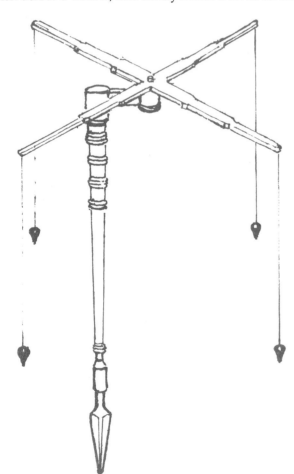, (p.19). This involved first of all clearing a broad stretch of terrain, then cutting the turf to lay the foundations and getting used to handling the various materials that will be used. Then they measured the site with rods and surveyed it with what was known as a *groma*, []. Valens was amazed that the unnerringly straight roads they built from one end of the country to the other were made possible by such a simple device. The *groma* was set firmly on the ground and adjusted until its plumb-lines were perfectly perpendicular; the four arms could then be used to calculate a straight line or a rectangle.

By now Felix has ordered the trainee soldiers to return to the wooden dummy for more weapon practice, this time with the javelin. In order to strengthen the arms, the javelins used in training are heavier than those normally carried. At long last, after several hours of intensive and exhausting exercises, Felix dismisses the young men and they make their way back to barracks, ravenous for a meal and some relaxation.

THE EVENING'S ACTIVITIES

Before we find out how Valens spends his evenings don't let us forget Longinus, the night-sentry who has gone to spend his day off with Regina and their two children in the cottage in the *vicus*. In fact he has spent the morning in a deep sleep on a pile of ferns covered in a blanket. Regina has sent the children out to play not to wake their father while she gets on with the cleaning and preparing the food.

Regina is one of the local Silures. She was brought up in one of the valleys north of Isca, where her parents farmed and sold what little they produced to the Romans. When she reached marrying age (around 15), she turned her sights on Isca, as all the Silurian girls did. After all, the soldiers had money — a rare commodity among the Silures — and they looked strong, vigorous young men. She realises she cannot be Longinus' lawful wife until his military service is completed, but she is content to live with him in the hope that he will not be sent to serve somewhere else.

Regina knows full well that her modest dwelling can hardly compare with the living quarters enjoyed by the **legatus**, but it is better than the hovels her own people live in, in the valleys. There are some Silures, it is true, who lead a pretty easy life in Venta, but Regina is quite content with her lot and the security it gives her.

[] A *groma*.

So she sweeps the hard, earthen floor with a will and arranges the red and black crockery on the shelves. A piece of salted young goat-meat is roasting slowly in the oven. It is difficult to obtain fresh meat in March, but Regina has added herbs to the pot to improve the taste. She then begins kneading dough to make bread, which will not turn out like the lighter loaves we buy today but more like unleavened bread of the kind baked on a griddle.

Regina wears a simple tunic, but she has a pretty bronze brooch on her shoulder, bronze rings on her fingers, and a bone pin in her hair. Longinus bought some of these for her, and the others she purchased for herself in the market. Market-day in the *vicus* is always a red-letter day for Regina and her neighbours. Merchants come from far off, some with dark skins from distant countries, to peddle all kinds of things in the market: jewllery, pottery, sweatmeats, material for making clothes and shoes and what have you. Some Silurian merchants are there too, selling wool, meat, livestock, sheep- and goat-skins, leather, fish and ale. With the money that Longinus gives her Regina enjoys looking around the market, though she knows she has to be prudent as they are not well-off.

Regina is about 25 years old with an eight year-old son and a six year-old daughter. She will not live to be very old: most women die before they reach forty. In coming to live with Longinus she has made an effort to learn Latin in order to converse with him more easily, but she is still more fluent in her own tongue, Brythonic. This is the language she uses with her parents, who are still alive, and with her own people whom she sees in the market. She also speaks it to her children when Longinus is not at home, but it is a Brythonic that is already different from the language she herself learnt as a child because there are now so many Latin words in it. Some of these tend to slip into her own speech after she has been talking with Longinus about his work, words like *fossa, porta, pontem* and *castellum*; and others come up in discussion about the cottage, like *fenestra, murus, parietem* and *stabellum*.

As for Longinus, he is a soldier of course, and as such is under the authority of the *legatus* who in turn is a servant of the Emperor. Since Regina is not officially Longinus's wife she is not subject to the *legatus* but she has to recognize the authority of the Council of the *vicus*, whose members are called *vicanorum magistri*. Their duties include keeping a register of the population and of those among them who pay taxes, maintaining the streets in good condition, making arrangements for the market and stipulating where exactly refuse may be tipped and corpses buried. There are times when the Council has to obey the *legatus*, especially on those occasions when the inhabitants of the *vicus* trespass on army property. This is a real problem because the population of the *vicus* is growing, and with the adults and children together there could well be more people living in the *vicus* than in the fort.

Although we have been concentrating on Regina, who is typical of most of the women who live with soldiers, many of the inhabitants of the *vicus* are men. They include retired soldiers, shopkeepers, bakers, labourers, leather-workers, carpenters, smiths and wagon-drivers, as well as the small farmers, gardeners and charcoal burners who work in the locality. These are all trying to eke out a living and raise families but they do not have the security of income that a soldier enjoys. They have to work or starve. There is no unemployment benefit or sick-pay or old age pension.

When Longinus wakes in the early afternoon Regina is spinning on a loom, using thread she has made herself and coloured with a purple dye she bought in the market. She is making a cloak for herself. But when she sees that Longinus is awake she starts preparing a meal and seeing to his needs.

Their conversation is that of man and wife in every age. Can they afford to send their small son to the new little school in the *vicus* run by a travelling teacher? Longinus would like him to improve his Latin so that he too can join the army when he is older. Longinus also wants to buy a hunting dog, but Regina would rather spend the money on some crockery. She tells him that the roof is leaking just above where the children sleep, so Longinus spends the rest of the afternoon repairing it.

As the day turns to dusk Regina puts the children to bed and Longinus heads for the tavern nearby to meet his friends from the barracks. He spends an hour or so with them drinking mulled wine and playing dice in the gloaming. Their talk is mainly of military matters — the centurion's quick temper, who will get the job of *signifer* (standard-bearer) in the unit once Quintus retires, and the usual grumble at the amount deducted from their wages to pay for clothes, food and weapons. Eventually Longinus returns to the cottage to sleep, but he will have to get back to barracks by daybreak to join the ranks in readiness for another day's work.

While Longinus was in the tavern Valens has had a meal of meat and bread and gone with some companions to the large bath-house near the hospital. They pass through a colonnade to a door which opens into a large hall whose massive roof is supported by more columns. The air is full of the grunts and exclamations of men engaged in physical exercise, individually and in groups, Others lie out on tables as servants massage their limbs. Regulus, the **primus pilus** (the legion's chief centurion) is one of those doing exercises: despite his sixty years and whitening hair, his body is still as tough as teak. As one of the most important men in the fort (*the* most important, in his own view) he is treated most respectfully by one and all. He will hold his position for a twelve month, then he will be given another important post in the legion.

During the summer these physical exercises are performed in the *palaestra*, the open-air gymnasium. There is a long outdoor swimming-pool at their disposal too, but it is too cold at this time of year. So Valens and his friends to go the *apodyterium* (changing room) where they undress and leave their clothes with the servant on duty.

Then they enter the *tepidarium*, a heated room where they are soon bathed in perspiration. There is no fire or heater of any kind to be seen but the floor and the walls are warm, thanks to an underground heating system that radiates hot air through channels under the floor and up the walls. After some time here, chatting about this and that just as Longinus and his friends were doing in the tavern, they move on to the *caldarium* where the sizzling room temperature makes them perspire freely. They rub themselves with oil and scrape the dirt from their skin with a bronze *strigilis* (scraper). Here too there is a servant at hand to knead and massage their flesh and their muscles.

Now invigorated, their bodies warm and tingling, they move on to the *frigidarium*, an unheated room where the cold hits them like a knife. Here there is a cold water plunge-bath, and with a shout each soldier in turn jumps in, before drying and getting dressed. What would the Romans, who liked to spend hours on end — sometimes a whole day — in the baths, make of today's habit of a quick two-minute shower? For it is actually dark by the time Valens makes his way back to barracks; the stars are out and the frost is glistening on the ground.

So ends a typical day in the lives of two typical soldiers in the fort at Isca. They have not had to face any danger nor has there been any real excitement, which is perhaps surprising in view of the fact that these are fighting men. Yet such, for the most part, is the sort of life led by a Roman soldier.

JULIUS VALENS

The day we have described in the lives of Longinus and Valens has been an imaginary one, and Longinus is imaginary too. But there actually *was* a soldier in Caerleon named Julius Valens, and his gravestone has survived, bearing the following inscription: K

K

DIS MANIBUS
IULIUS VALENS VETERANUS
LEGIONIS II AUGUSTAE VIXIT
ANNIS C IULIA
SECUNDINA CONIUNX
ET IULIUS MARTINUS FILIUS
FACIENDUM CURAVERUNT

Translated this says:

To the Gods of the Dead
Julius Valens
veteran soldier of the Second Augustan Legion
who lived for one hundred years
Julia Secundina, his wife
and Julius Martinus, his son
erected this stone in his memory
(literally, saw to the making of this work)

This is remarkable evidence of a man — the only one we know of — who lived to a hundred years of age in the Roman period. By luck his wife's gravestone has survived too, L. He may have married her after retiring from the army.

L

DIS MANIBUS ET
MEMORIAE
IULIAE SECUNDINAE
MATRI PIISSIMAE VIXIT
ANNIS LXXV: GAIUS IULIUS
FACIENDUM CURAVIT

Matri piissimae means 'his most dutiful mother'. Can you complete the translation of this inscription with the help of the first one?

3. ROMAN SITES TO VISIT

Most of us in Wales live within fairly easy reach of Roman sites and of museums that exhibit Roman antiquities. They are well worth visiting. Some sites can disappoint since often there is little to see, but mentioned below are places that are not only important but really interesting to see as well. Remember that there is more to it than just the remains that happen to be still visible. You might ask yourself, Why did the Romans choose this particular location? They would have considered several factors, and given high priority to security, links with other camps, the road network and the water supply.

ROMAN SITES

BRECON

Y Gaer is situated a few miles outside. Follow the A40 for four miles west out of Brecon and turn right towards Aberbrân. At Aberbrân turn right again and carry straight on for two miles until you reach a crossroads. Turn back hard right along a track that leads to Y Gaer farm.

CARDIFF

The outer walls of Cardiff Castle are a reasonable reconstruction of the original Roman fort.

CAERLEON

North of Newport. One of the three legionary

A The north gate of Cardiff Castle.

British forts. The walls, bath-house, barracks and amphitheatre can still be seen. There is also a museum.

CAER-WENT

A town on the A48 between Newport and Chepstow. The impressive south walls may be walked, and the foundations of the temple and a few houses are still visible. Compare these remains with Alan Sorrell's artist's reconstruction of the original shops and houses. B

B

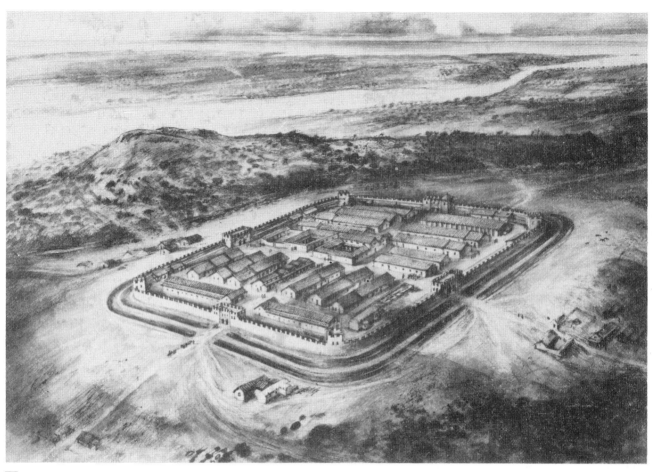

C

SEGONTIUM

The fort and museum are alongside the road from Caernarfon to Waunfawr before reaching Llanbeblig church. C is another artist's impression by Alan Sorrell, this time of Segontium.

OTHER SITES IN WALES

There are several other sites that are rather less impressive than those above but which are still well worth seeing. The figures in brackets refer to Ordnance Survey Maps 1 : 2500. A list would include Gelli-gaer (ST 1397), Neath (SS 7497), Castell Collen (SO 0562), Dolau Cothi (SN 6640), Caer Gai (SH 8731), Caerhun (SH 7770), Holyhead (SH 2482) and the Amphitheatre at Carmarthen on the A40 near Priory Close, Tomen y Mur near Trawsfynydd in Gwynedd is rewarding, but its location is very remote.

MUSEUMS

In addition to the museums at Caerleon and Segontium there are fascinating collections of Roman exhibits in the National Museum of Wales in Cardiff, Newport Museum, Brecon Museum, Dyfed Museum in Abergwili and Llandrindod Museum.

ROMAN SITES IN ENGLAND

There are some extremely important English sites that are also within fairly easy reach of Wales. In the north of England there is the Grosvenor Museum in Chester, in the Midlands, Rowley's House Museum in Shrewsbury, and a museum at Wroxeter on the site of the remains at Viroconium. In southern England the Corinium Museum is at Chichester, and there is a *villa* at Chedworth just to the north of it. Bath (Aquae Sulis) is within easy reach of South Wales and there, and at Hadrian's Wall, you will see the most impressive of all the Roman remains in Britain.

4. QUESTIONS

1. Look at the map of Roman Wales (on page 1) and place it alongside a map of Wales today. What are the modern names for the following places: Isca (the fort), Isca (the river), Venta, Burrium, Cicucium, Nidum, Leucarum?

2. What other tribes apart from the Silures lived in Wales?

3. What do you think of Roman medicine? What is your opinion of Andronicos as a doctor?

4. What is Aquae Sulis called today? What do you know about it in Roman times?

5. On page 21 are some of the Latin words that found their way into Regina's Celtic language. Do they remind you of any Welsh words with which you may be familiar? What is their English meaning?

6. The Welsh words *cell* (cell), *carchar* (prison), *cadwyn* (chain), *fflangell* (whip) and *caeth* (captive) all come from the Latin. What do you think they tell us about the nature of the Roman occupation of Wales?

7. You remember that Secundina became Valens' wife. Assuming that she was a Celt, write an imaginary conversation between her and Regina. What do they talk about? What do they think about the lives they now lead? What have they got to say about their husbands, their homes and the Roman army?

5. GLOSSARY

Amphitheatre — a round or oval-shaped open space surrounded by rising tiers of seats. The most thoroughly excavated amphitheatre in Britain is that at Caerleon.

Armoury — a place where weapons (arms) are kept and sometimes made.

Auxiliary — a soldier, but not a legionary (see below), in the Roman army.

Centurion — the commander of a century.

Century — a company of 80 soldiers.

Chronological order — arranged in sequence according to age or date.

Civitas — a tribe and its territory.

Fort — an enclosed and fortified stronghold. In Caerleon a rampart, a ditch and walls protected the soldiers who lived inside the fort.

Legatus — the commander of a legion and governor of a province.

Legion — a division of 4,000 – 6,000 soldiers who were Roman citizens.

Legionary — a soldier in a legion.

Mosaic — pictures or patterns produced by cementing together pieces of stone or glass of various colours.

Primus pilus — the chief centurion of a legion (literally, 'first javelin').

Province — land under Roman occupation, outside Italy.

Via sagularis — the road that ran all round the fort in the space between the defensive walls and the internal buildings (literally, the 'cloak street').

Vine-staff — a short cane carried by an officer, often used to inflict punishment. Also known as a swagger-stick.